Raising Eden

Wisdom of the Eternal

by

Daniel Dunn

Dedication

This Book is dedicated to all of the people / beings whose lives have been claimed by the Predator energies of the darkness & by the monstrosity that is the Beast System of Babylon. To all those without voices, and all the souls who have been lost without a trace. May the love, grace and guidance of God The Creator shine upon you always, lighting the path, so you can find your way home, back to yourselves. You will all be remembered forever within our eternal memory.

INTRODUCTION

TRANSCEND THE INFINITIES

Open your mind, open your heart, get ready to be in relationship with your higher self, and embody your Greater Deeper Mind.

FEEL THE LOVE OF GOD THE CREATOR, for this is WISDOM OF THE ETERNAL, and it was meant for you.

This wisdom is collected from a decade of communications with the divine. Some days one piece of wisdom was received, sometimes a few, sometimes none. But always with purpose, the revelation is still on-going.

This divine communication is specifically received for you to aid you into your own power, help you refine your state of being, and free you up to evolve into your True Greater Self. So you can then be an embodiment of your True Self within the world.

Read One Wisdom Quote per day, exercise your powers of patience, consistency, perseverance and discipline.

Stay with and repeat the quote, plus your thoughts about it to yourself, throughout the day as many times as you like.

Whether you are busy or not is irrelevant as long as you have focus upon what is said that day and it is the main focal point for your thoughts.

Abide with the quote and be with the quote. OWN IT!

Reflect deeply upon each quote; let it imbue its being, its living energy and its wisdom into your being. Let it dissolve its divine essence and energies into your consciousness, to become a part of you forever.

Plant endless seeds in the fertile soils, of mind, dark matter & mystery. For ye will surely reap the bountiful harvest of endless beauty, divine splendour and power, as you become who you know you truly already are & Eden Is raised within, so it can be reflected into the world.

Good journey to Self.

BE LOVE

"BE L((((O))))VE"

*"By the **will** & **power of one**, shall **all** or nothing be done"*

"**LOVE**, **(L)**iving **(O)**ne **(V)**ibrational **(E)**nergy"

"LOVE.

It is called this, not only because Love is one, but because it is a living consciously aware energy and is alive"

"Love is not just a word,

*but **a living conscious force**"*

"*In order to survive, one must have Love.* **In order to thrive**, *they must have* **Self-Love**"

"In Love all possibilities exist to be manifest in any moment, it is the highest purest frequency in existence from where **all things are birthed** and **gain life**"

*"**Love** is the **secret to LIFE**"*

"To Love unconditionally, gives you the keys to create any reality and deal with any situation in any moment"

*"The Love within You Burns Hotter than **a Trillion suns**"*

"Live Love,

be Love"

"The ultimate expression of the creator is life, and the secret to life is Love. Some say God is Love but life is Love as well'

*"Love is the **master key**, to forge your destiny and create an empowered, pure, Singular consciousness within"*

"Each day remind yourself, the Love that binds us is far more important than the power we wield"

*"Fear is of the **finite mind**,*

*Love is of the **infinite heart**"*

"Fear destroys possibilities and thus limits your options, the more in fear you are the more your life contracts and possibilities are destroyed. The more you Love the more your life expands and possibilities become available"

"To be love and occupy your -self is no new age or hippy philosophy; it is simultaneously the easiest thing to do and the hardest in this world. It requires the most strength & integrity"

"In love and compassion you are actually expanding into more of yourself, thus your soul is freed, and liberated, and you have full actualization"

"Love is like a shadow, chase it and it will always dissolve, BE STILL & you can drink of its waters for all time"

"Love conquers all and the only real truth is infinity of Love"

"Do not be afraid to Love, for all is one and in the end all that exists is Love"

"Love makes you strong; it creates PRESENCE which in turn creates & births LIFE".

"To LOVE is to be PRESENT,

to be PRESENT is to LOVE,

*for **LOVE is PRESENCE**"*

"Review your Day, every single day without question, this reflection in of itself will make you Powerful. Repeat, Repeat & Repeat once more, discard all that was bad and did not serve you, while rejoice in all that was good"

"Raise the New Eden by becoming what we were born to be, LOVE"

"In the seeming absence of The Creators Love, all questions arise. Yet in the presence of The Creators Love, all questions dissolve"

"God is the most powerful force in existence from which all things birth, arise and have life. Everything is from God and of God. God is the powerful Attractor pulling everything towards itself indefinitely. God is STILL. Everything else is IN MOTION"

*"The **POWER OF LOVE** within you is so powerful it **CAN HEAL ANYTHING**, including your future."*

"Within Creation, ALL ARE ONE. There is only one Being here. At the highest level of creation and even beyond that, there is only UNITY. This **L.**iving **O.**ne **V.**ibrational **E.**nergy (LOVE & ONESS), LAW OF UNITY is written into light, into the heart of reality itself and into the heart of all things. You must come to understand it is not a manmade law and it is the only true law of GOD THE CREATOR.

This vibrant living ocean of pure love consciousness, decided to manifest itself into all things, vibrations and forms. Thus the ultimate truth lies in complete absence of itself; it is an emptiness, yet a fullness of being"

"You do not need any external dogma to walk with The Creator in any moment. The truth requires no manmade doctrines, religions, churches or scripts. It does not require anything external. There is no such thing as a holy book, because THE LIVING TRUTH is alive and well within you, and every fibre of your being, thus the truth is irrelevant and dead outside oneself. Understanding God The Creator's total unity is all you need to master to a high degree to reconnect with your true identity, Deeper Mind and Higher True Self"

"You are living in an

ELECTRO-MAGNETIC,

FRACTAL-INFINITY,

HOLOGRAPHIC ENERGY MATRIX

OF THE ONE *"*

"Take all the things you think you know and forget it all. Do not hold onto any

pre-conceived notions. Dissolve it all in the dimension of the heart, for the HEART IS INFINITE and the human surface EGO MIND is to limited to go where we are going. You will then be a little bit closer to the truth of things"

"Think through your infinite heart and be aware, Knowing is of the mind and finite illusion. AWARENESS is of THE INFINITE HEART"

"Remember the perceived outside universe and world exists only to cultivate and enrich your inner truth, not to hold onto anything as belief, THAT only serves to limit your perception"

*"You will Be what you believe,

you can BE anything"*

"TRANSCEND THE INFINITIES; it is in the REALMS OF THE MYSTERY AND THE GREAT UNKNOWN where you will find your answers."

"Be brave,

Be strong,

Be courageous,

BE LOVE"

"Always base your spirituality upon your own experience, not fairy tales, fantasy or imagination. For it is the strongest foundation in existence to build upon and nobody can take away your experience"

"AWARENESS THROUGH EXPERIENCE, EXPERIENCE THROUGH AWARNESS."

"On a microcosmic and macrocosmic level stretching to infinity, WE ARE ALL ONE. Everybody around you is a reflection of yourself, they are your teachers, as you are theirs. Do you want to harm another now, knowing THEY ARE A PART OF YOU?

I didn't think so ;-)"

"Understanding The LAW OF THE UNITY OF ALL THINGS can heal everything upon every level, and bring everything to full resolution. It is HIGHER CONSCIOUSNESS OF SELF, ITSELF that will HEAL THIS WORLD, the human Condition and ALL THINGS. The biggest problem within this world is no Self-awareness, people do bad because they cannot see. All IS, WAS, AND WILL ALWAYS BE ONE"

"Everything is a reflection,

Thus the Love that is denied,

Is the pain that's carried inside"

"Everything that is, was, and will be

Is part of one original thought,

Produced by one original SOUND."

"We are infinite, there is no end to what we can create or become. Our understanding is infinite, our journey is infinite, what we can create and accomplish alone or together is infinite, our perception of The Creation and our ability to create reality is infinite. That which is infinite cannot be separate, for separateness is mind illusion and is a finite conception. In UNITY there is infinity, within an Infinite Creator, there exists only UNITY OF BEING. Thus we are the VERY LIVING DREAMER OF OURSELVES"

"What you create, you get.

The Universe is indiscriminate"

"By identifying with Our Surface Ego Human Mind, living in Illusions such as Fear and perceived separateness, resisting our hearts Inner Divine guidance, our True Greater Deeper Mind and true identity. It allows us to distort reality in varying ways and to varying degrees. However this distortion in consciousness is not necessary at all and only brings great harm and destruction to oneself, others, and the world"

"The Truth is. We are everything that IS, ever was and ever will be. We are every Thought, every emotion, every Being, every event, every circumstance, every situation,

EVERY POSSIBILITY.

We are the totality of the whole and are

INFINITE UNITY IN ACTION,

AWAKEN TO YOUR FULL INFINITE POTENTIAL!!"

"STILLNESS.

You are the stillness at the centre of your being.

BE STILL"

"Everything is one; this is your True Self identity. Only then will your infinite potential be tapped and the flood gates opened. Because the only limits are those we choose to create upon ourselves"

"There is nothing outside of yourself that is not already contained within. The Wizard in Oz knows of this well"

"Do not fear the future

or you will have no room left,

*to **imagine the beauty of the NOW**"*

"Walk the path of infinite expansion, moment by moment"

"Reality is not a solid state like most perceive, it is an ever changing state of fluidity, forever reshaping, reforming & re-creating itself"

"I think one person can change the entire system for everything and everyone, because we are connected to the system"

"What you do in this moment is all that truly matters, this book is a catalyst for your own remembrance"

"Take everything you think you know, turn it inside out and expand it infinitely in all directions, you will then be a little bit closer to the truth"

"Everything you think you know must be left at the doors of the temple, before one can enter"

"One must serve something Greater than what ideas of one self is. Only by giving yourself to something greater than yourself will you increase your integrity exponentially, thus create stability and then ultimately Unity of Self."

"We have infinite power and potential from any point, in any moment or reality"

"Infuse into your being the core purpose, THE SPIRITUAL NECESSITY TO EVOLVE"

"Find your reality and create it in each moment with all of your heart, every fibre of your being and through the power of love"

"Do not look outside yourself for truth, only look into the world for paths to your own inner truth"

"All truth is within; do not look into the illusionary world for truth. Learn to follow the divine part of yourself,

Establish a relationship with your Higher True Self within and follow its guidance, allow it to teach you, in essence You become your own teacher"

"It is paramount that you create and cultivate daily, a singular truth within and embody it"

"We exist in a reality created from our dreams and imagination, where our imagination is far more important than our knowing"

"Question every basic truth and

Create yourself in every moment"

"Do not serve limitation; create your own pathway of awakening with your Higher True Self and without limitation"

"The torments and desperation we suffer are fruits of the misplaced faith we have deposited in this programme of limitation of Self"

"All the problems on this earth are caused by people thinking they are limited, thus there is suppression of their true expression."

"The root cause of all prime distortion in this universe and any reality is caused by perceived separation from one another, the universe and most notably, God The Creator. When ultimately there is no separation"

"Like matter itself, we are infinite in all directions. Only true cultivation of you owning your divinity and infinity, plus your belief in it, will set you free"

*"Embody **Fractal Infinity**, now is the time to be what you already are"*

"Light up the world and

Let the darkness dissolve

*in the **beauty of your vision**"*

"Be infinite, we are one"

"Open your mind,

know your power,

be as water"

"As you get older you learn more and it becomes an on-going thing, even now my whole being never stops it's like a path that's infinite, you just carry on learning, Refining yourself, and expanding your awareness. There's no stopping it because that's what infinity is"

"Think in terms of everything being alive in this conscious living universe. This Creation is alive, music, movies, thoughts, matter itself, and even the space we live within and have our being. Everything has a life of its own, it is designed with purpose. Thus Our Creations have a life of their own and must be set free. They must be allowed to evolve, to breathe and live, for they too are growing in awareness, and allowing something to be what it is truly meant to be, is one of the greatest acts of love one can demonstrate"

"An ocean of vibrant living consciousness exists inside each and every one of us. Connect to it and let it Glow, Let it Flow, THAT is your power and Greater Life"

"You are not your body, You are an **INFINITE ETERNAL BEING OF LOVE"**

"You are the wave and you are the ocean. You are one with the universe and everything around you, the universe is your body. This is the TRUE PRIME DEFINITION OF SELF"

"Free your mind. Open your heart. You are equal to all people / beings and are at peace with this. You do not believe you are better than anybody else or a God or a God over them. Thus In the embodiment of your TRUE IDENTITY, no God complex is formed. The Ego is in true relationship and serves your Greater Deeper Mind, it no longer dominates your life or actions"

"You must come to know and be aware that, one who truly knows The Self & what it means, will not try to dominate anybody external to themselves in anyway. For they are aware, they are THE WHOLE ENERGY FIELD (Wave & Ocean)"

"Only those who define the self as the body will seek domination over others, because of the fear of feeling separate and of not having a True Self Identity"

"Knowing what you ARE or ARE NOT

Is one of the biggest mis-conceptions within our world"

"One of the reasons religious peoples say ONENESS is Luciferian or new age BS is they do not have a True Self Identity and are disempowered, they do not fully understand what oneness means and its ability to heal the earth of all evil"

"Being one and living under your TRUE IDENTITY does not mean you have a Borg Collective or Hive mentality and lose your individualism. Only people who have a false sense of Self or have completely misunderstood think such things because that is where their MIRROR OF PERCEPTION is aligned. With the false perception that they are their body and their thoughts.

BEING ONE actually means you are truly infinitely empowered, individual and unique. A catalyst for positive change and infinitely, different from the next person as infinity itself (unconditioned and free from being programmed). With the Full SPECTRUM OF POSSIBILITY AND CREATIVITY at your disposal at any moment, to be a High degree master in any reality, or moment, and to re-program yourself and the waves around you as you see fit. It also means you have FULL CORE INTEGRITY and cannot be controlled, suppressed, or deceived. For you have not created a space within for external forces to fill and you have taken full responsibility for yourself on all levels and dimensions. NO POWER IS GIVEN AWAY"

"ALIGNED with your TRUE IDENTITY OF ONENESS WITH ALL THINGS, you are the worst nightmare for those who seek domination and power over others. So Do not let a few people with a warped sense of Self, deter you from being what your truly already are. You are an INFINITELY POWERFUL ETERNAL BEING OF LOVE"

"Master your own consciousness to a high degree and you will master the world to a high degree, but first one must accept the reality in which they find themselves and positively construct from that point forwards. Just having the potential is not enough; it is the doing each day, bit by bit, piece by piece, step by step, that is the most important ingredient"

"EVERYTHING IS CONSCIOUSNESS.

What a person or Being pays attention to, they become Conscious of.

CREATION IS OUR ALLIE, **USE IT**"

"Be the architect of your own accomplishments, do not be the observer in your own life. Actively participate.

OWN IT"

"Direct everything with inside yourself in your life, direct your thoughts, direct your emotions, direct your time, direct your energy, and direct your destiny.

BE AT ONE"

"Many people will say what you need to hear, but they will never take action on what they preach. It is time you place your faith in actions and not in words"

"A True relationship is not chosen by the mind of the person, it is found in the

Heart of the Engagement"

"Do not try to control others in any way, shape or form. Only control yourself from moment to moment, and how you respond in the situation you find yourself within"

"The only way things will change, is if you take responsibility for yourself on all levels, Empower yourself from within, You are the thing you seek. Simply refine what you already are and have the potential to be, we are all Students and Teachers"

"Being truly sensitive to your Divine Spark within, Your Deeper Greater Mind and Higher True Self. One can FEEL all possible energy potential of something, a person or an event from the outset. One can know the outcome of relationship from the outset and thus can dive in the deep end fearlessly"

"When listening to and following your Deeper Greater Mind and Higher True Self, what looks like craziness, chaos and random to some, is an ACT OF CERTAINTY within yourself"

"Follow your heart , with your full might. Do not let others dissuade you from what you know to be and what you know is true"

"There is Always Hope, when The Creators Children Decide to be a Force for Good within the World. It is this very thing, the brave, the courageous, the wise, the creators, and the lovers have. That keeps the sacred spark of light shining for all life and all God's creatures".

"Friends are Companions, who help, support, nurture, amplify and enhance the experiences in the journey to Self, on the path of life"

"GREAT WORKS are the product of GREAT RELATIONSHIPS"

"The more you practice the better you get, when something works, repeat it and use it. Mastery to any high degree takes time, but even then there are no true masters within this world, for mastery is saved for when we go to the next domain"

"Most people are in wrong relationship with themselves, they think they are their MIND, and that their thoughts are their own"

"To get everything,

one must give everything.

For that is what true relationship is"

"Everything is simple, people themselves complicate things"

"You are stronger than your emotion, direct them and do not allow them to direct you"

"You need POWER to do anything. Power is not evil. Do not be afraid of power. Do not give your power away on any level. God gave you POWER to do good and be good. Apply it, apply yourself everyday"

"Do not fear power. That is one of the biggest mistakes within this world. The lie that Power is evil or a bad thing is what has propelled the world into its current state. The criminals got organized first as they sought power over life and the good did not. It is now time for a world in which the good get organized and exorcize the Power that The Creator gave them, to be guardians and stewards of this world. It is time for the good to get organized as good as or better than the bad."

"Take on the responsibility that is thrust upon you by the world that you did not plan for. Great beings never seek power, it is gifted to them naturally and without mind. Own it, be it, have total respect for it and use it wisely. When it is restrained by your Higher True Self and Greater Deeper Mind then it will not be self-destructive, nor will it bring harm to neither the world nor others, it is only ever then, a force of healing and good"

"Potential is not power until focused, applied and manifest. POWER is determined by how much energy you can move from one domain to another"

"You do not always need to know where you are going, as long as you apply each day in life and each moment, what you do know"

"Do not allow your experiences to claim you, Claim them"

"The true measure of intelligence in this universe, is adapting quickly within changing circumstances"

"A wise being will hear and attain itself unto wise counsels"

"People can teach you one of two things, what to do and what not to do. Contrast in learning is a good thing and speeds up your growth and evolution; it is like a quantum leap forwards for you on your journey. But make sure you use the discernment of your Greater Deeper Mind and Higher Self to tell the difference, or you are doomed to repeat their mistakes also"

"Cultivate REAL FREEDOM

Through the awareness of TRUTH"

"EVERYTHING IS RELATIONSHIP.

God The Creator is the Total sum

of ALL Relationship"

"Every challenge is an Opportunity to grow"

"The most loving thing that one can do for another human being, is not to give them things to think about. But to bring to the surface and awaken the gifts that are already within them"

"Don't be swept up by the allure of the moment, only a fool reacts, a wise soul responds"

"Necessity dictates the amount of recklessness we must undertake"

"My personal feelings are overshadowed by my blossoming destiny and soul responsibility to follow it"

"How can one try to control another, when one cannot even control their own thoughts from moment to moment?"

"You must take action to reflect the truths of what you say, or they are but hollow words"

"Life is a reflection of what we allow ourselves to see"

"Truth is a journey we all must take alone, we can look on the outside for paths to our own inner truth, and we can read books to gain new insights and meet people who can guide us to see the truth within. Yet one must simply look within and use the heart, the Higher, Deeper, Greater Mind to know truth from untruth"

"Everything is consciousness.

Everything is a communication.

Everything is vibration.

Everything is a relationship"

"Learn to channel your energy,

Energy creates. Energy destroys.

***Be mindful"*

*"Words have great power to heal or to destroy. **Be mindful**"*

"All of the actions you take in life and unresolved issues you create both consciously and unconsciously, will present themselves as Fate in the future, if you do not deal with them in the present. People Bind themselves to the fate they make"

"DO NOT follow any outside force or influence, definitely no Galactic Federation, Ashtar Command, or any self-proclaimed ascended master. Follow no named or labelled group, or you will leave yourself open to all deception."

"Use your intuition, or should I say your inner teacher. Inner-Tuition (Your Heart). For it is the voice of The Creator living within you, the divine spark and your Greater True Deeper Mind"

"Truth within This world is a filtered experience"

"In our earth Anti-Civilization it tells you from birth that you are limited, are separate from God, and you are your body. This is so people live under the FALSE IDENTITY, and so perceive the world and themselves through this Personal Mind Illusion. This is because THE ARCHITECTS OF THIS ANTI-CIVILIZATION / SYSTEM want you to be disempowered and to control you. That is why the world is Centered around MATERIALISM.

Let go of your Ego, let go of the idea that your body is you, that your Mind is you. Because not knowing the TRUE SELF creates all evil within this world and is the PRIME ROOT CAUSE. Let your HEART (Greater Deeper Mind) dominate your destiny, never let the Personal Mind or its shadow, the Ego, dominate the TRUE SELF."

"Cultivating a SINGULAR TRUTH WITHIN can solve all problems on Earth, heal the Earth fully, and bring all paradoxes to conclusion. For all problems on Earth can easily be solved in the Higher Dimensions with Higher Consciousness"

"It is the mark of true strength

to maintain a beautiful loving heart,

in a cruel heartless world"

"Revolutions come around and around binding humanity in circles and chains; it is time for **EVOLUTION**, for that lasts for all time"

"Money does not work; it splinters consciousness into two divides, those who have and those who have not".

*"Do not allow culture (ure-cult) to become your cult. Create culture, **we are culture**"*

"Only when those who love peace can organize as good as or better than those who love war, will there be peace"

"There is always a risk with each expansive endeavour"

"Whenever or wherever you hit barriers or are stopped by outer forces when looking at information, THAT is the place to start, that is where you will find the REAL TREASURE"

"In order to know the truth of seemingly random or chaotic events and to understand them, one must only ask themselves one question; Who benefited?"

"We are a world of magicians and

i-magi-nation

is the link to our unlimited power"

"We need critical thinkers,

not to be critical of thinking"

'The Nazi-Germans said, 'Work sets you free', but it's only half true. Works sets you free Yes, but it's not when it's working for somebody else, it's when it's working for your True Self, your own goal and God given purpose, you are free while you are fulfilling your true destiny"

"The purpose of war is to disrupt or destroy all communication of those you wish to conquer"

"The COMING INVASION is set to coincide with the coming economic implosion, the money system that was DESIGNED TO FAIL FROM ITS INCEPTION"

"Corruption ANYWHERE, is Corruption EVERYWHERE"

"The BIGGER THE SYSTEM the longer it takes to change"

"The dark forces within our world, and forces from beyond it, FEAR US. That is why they do the monstrous things they do. Our LIGHTNESS and BEINGNESS is far more powerful than they are"

"People need to observe the native tribes, the indigenous tribes, because they have lived for thousands of years, in balance, they know how to look after the world.

Already, they have the Knowledge"

"People need to give up everything if they want everything"

"Thousands of people dying every year and wars all over the place, that's not a normal state of affairs for the world. Human beings are supposed to be peaceful, they are supposed to be on a higher level, not to bring harm to others. They are supposed to be stewards of the earth"

*"It does not matter whether or not things are illusion, imagined, or unreal,
once they are believed in or applied in life,
THEY BECOME REAL"*

"Dark Forces within the world are aware energy is needed to create any reality or hologram matrix, for everything is consciousness. THUS FOCUS OF ONE OF MORE BEINGS BECOMES REALITY"

"The Movie and Music industries are completely controlled by fraternal orders and have long since been bought up. By the SELF PROCLAIMED ELITE, on their quest for power and complete domination of humanity"

"People haven't cultivated peace within themselves so they'll never attain peace in the world, because the world is a reflection. If they want peace it has to Start with themselves"

*"The Stronger one is,

the Stronger we all are"*

"He who controls the past, also controls the future, for we are but a reflection"

*"He who does not learn from his mistakes, is sure to repeat them. **Fate is binding**"*

"What you think you know of the world is corrupted and anything of importance hidden from you purposely"

"The system in this world is not built to enslave you, it is built so **people enslave themselves**"

"It is a system built to maintain the status quo, through fear and the power of the negative aspects of a person when they are stuck within Ego (Shallow Surface Human Mind) consciousness"

"Governments create massive events to sway there populations opinion in their favour at key times and nodal points within history, they manufacture this new history in their favour"

"Do not shrink from responsibility, rise to all challenges and conquer them responsibly. Responsibility creates security, thus security creates safety and freedom. Freedom and responsibility go hand in hand"

"Responsibility is not a burden, it is a vital ingredient and is a KEY OF FREEDOM. Guard it well, for freedom is rare within this universe"

"Look into every expression of truth no matter what form the energy takes; Religion, History, Geometry, Psychology, Science, Geography, Mathematics, to name but a few. Truth must be placed together for they each represent an expression of energy telling you a story and Only the whole will tell you the story of the whole energy field"

"All subjects are really one and it's only the component of Ego Surface Mind that creates division for humans."

"Everything is one jigsaw piece of the whole picture; otherwise its expression would not be there"

"Everybody has one piece of the jigsaw, so all must come together freely and share, let us build this picture together"

"The architects of this world have set the system up to try to make you a slave and prisoner to your own Ego (Human Mind), and limit your full conscious power (Infinite Heart)"

"Know that the chasm between the truth of reality, the universe, and what you have been told in all things, is so large it's almost unimaginable"

"Light is precious it must be safe guarded at all costs, the world will do everything it can to try to beat it from you because it fears it, those who desire control made it so. It is our spiritual integrity that is the most important thing to cultivate every day and keep, then use for the good of all, so protect it at all costs, for it is more valuable than you could ever know"

"Despite all you have been taught to think, light is not good and darkness bad. BOTH are a form of light and are neutral, in fact there are many, many forms of light. Those forces who dominate this world both human and other worldly, use all forms of Light as a weapon"

"This whole world civilization is built upon the foundation and energy expression of Ego consciousness and thus its life will be short. None of the world system is built by mistake; it is to keep you a slave and to disempower you."

"You have been asleep and born into a world of deception, it is time to establish a daily relationship with your Higher Self, awaken to your inner divine self, and align with your Greater Deeper True Mind"

"The surrendering to your Ego and chosen disconnect from your Higher Self and Deeper Greater True Mind, in essence is the rebellion against The Creator spoken of in the many religions"

"The Self Proclaimed ruling elite's deception against humanity exists mainly on a fundamental level, effecting aspects of reality which most people commonly and erroneously believe to be basic truths"

"Off world forces and their Shadow Government printing money out of thin air, continue to dominate this world, you must follow your destiny and take up your role. BE THE GUARDIAN OF ALL LIFE that you already deep down, know you are"

"THE UNIVERSE IS INFORMATION. So beware of those who deny you information, for in their hearts they desire to be your master"

"Fear and misdirection is the tool of the fallen ones, reality and appearance are different from one another in this civilization. The surface is shiny and gold, yet the core is rotten. It is a SMOKE AND MIRROR GAME "

"In this journey, it is how you get there that is most important, not the destination itself. Be mindful not to lose important things along the way."

"The sun is not a nuclear reactor, everything ever taught has been a lie. Because you have been looking in the wrong place and not accepting response-ability for yourself. Do not look outside yourself for answers but within, it is time to create everything from scratch and forget all you think you know. Live in FLUID AWARENESS and BE INFINITE like the fragment of the divine you are"

"To get anything done constructively in this world and dimension go from where you are right now, not where you were or want to be"

"There is only ONE RULE in Real True science and that is, THERE ARE NO RULES. For the moment you chose to create one, you splinter your own consciousness into more than one part. So a science with rules is not true to the Law of Unity and Oneness of The Creator. It is an illusion created only within the human mind like division and time itself. Truth does not fit perfectly into a box, it simply just IS"

"One world Religion = One World Government

One World Government = New World Order

New World Order IS The Alien Intervention!"

"We Live within a Culture of Death in this world, Become part of the

CULTURE OF LIFE"

"THE CHOICE IS YOURS.

Love & Peace

(Path of spirituality & connection)

 OR

Fear & War

(Path of technology & Disconnection!)"

"The Beast System is specifically designed to suck your ENERGY, limit your PERCEPTION OF REALITY and at all costs YOUR MULTIDIMENSIONALITY"

"In any system, dump it all. If you can create something better, CREATE IT, BUILD IT, LIVE IT"

"Most do not have the capacity for peace for they have not developed this aspect of themselves fully. A PEACE that lasts is not something you create overnight; it is a STATE OF BEING AND LIVING. One must first cultivate daily the capacity for peace, it is a lifelong refining process. You must put in the work daily and take direct action in this realm too see the world you wish to see. UNIFY within first and the worlds reflection will adjust unto thee"

"Let everything unfold at a natural pace, it has its own rhythm, everything has its own rhythm. Follow the example of God The Creator in its GREAT BENEVOLENCE, that is true wisdom"

"**God is the great attractor** which pulls everything towards itself indefinitely"

"Like cogs in a great machine, cycle within cycle, the whole of reality and creation is projected and constantly energized. All pulled by the will of the creator"

"Everything is One Unit of energy, connected to one Primary source"

"Everything outside yourself is also contained within, for we are one with all things and connected to the whole"

"Everything is One Unit of energy, everything is ONE.

Infinite potential, turned into infinite expression,

In a single moment of glory"

"There are two primary forces that make our universe what it is, both effects are birthed by the will of the creator. The first force is electrical and the second is magnetic. The Creator SELF had to isolate parts of its own energy to give rise to form. God the creator, created all vibrational form both material and immaterial from its own body. One could say God the creator did not create the universe, but rather became the universe"

"Magnetism allows all matter to exist and express itself; all matter creates a magnetic isolation field. This created space allows all form to live and exist in space time. This magnetic field makes the world feel dense/solid, and our isolated fields separate from one another, but we are really one"

"The two opposing forces of electro magnetism give rise to two birthed effects, we know and perceive them as time and gravity. Gravity is the movement of the energy flow (Projection) around a singularity core. It is the pulling of forces around a central singularity point indefinitely, gravity basically is law of attraction. An infinite pull of attraction towards a hyper-dimensional point (Singularity Core) beyond this universe. Like a cog being pulled, then a holographic projection into manifest form"

"Time is the duration of the light projection manifesting"

"Magnetism isolates manifestations and slows them down like a glue, time exists so all things do not seem to occur at once in this manifest reality"

"Time and gravity are illusions as all energy already exists and is expressing itself in one glorious Now moment"

"Every atom contains the potential energy and information of the whole universe and all of creation. It has infinite potential, just like you"

"Every atom has a singularity at its core; every human has a singularity at its core. Every planet, every star, every galaxy and the universe itself has a singularity at its core"

"All truth is within and within all things"

"We are one with everything, and have unlimited power and potential within"

"Everything is an expression and manifestation of energy, a symphony of vibration"

"The language of The Creator of all things, the Language of LIGHT, Has thus been revealed. Pure Communications, in vibrations themselves"

"All of the archetypes of sacred geometry hold specific vibrational energy potentials, which are all omnipresent omnipotent realities that are forever speaking to us about the true nature of The Creator, the Universe and all of Creation"

"Energy is but the movement of consciousness. The manifestations of energy as the symphony plays out, births all form, time, and dimension"

"The world and people are as yet unmade; one must simply fit the pieces together in the correct order"

"We are feathers in the wind able to blow where we wish, yet divinely guided at the same time"

"The Universe and Divine spark at the centre of your being is your teacher,

Live upon the wings of synchronicity"

"There is nothing out of place, no such thing as coincidence. It truly is cause and effect of one energy system interacting with another. This is the energy system the One created to give us free will, yet be on a divine path back to source."

"One person can directly affect the destiny of the entire universe, you must simply choose how you wish to express the energy you have been given".

"Never underestimate the power of stillness or the power of consistency, meditation creates stability and thus allows you to cope with anything, in any moment, or at any time"

"Man must know that his true power lies in the stillness of his centred self and not by the means in which he manifests that stillness"

"Knowledge like technology is neutral,

it's how we apply it that makes it good or bad"

"Realize your Potential power and send shockwaves through time"

"The universe is a living conscious being; it is expanding because its awareness is expanding"

"What is out there in the universe is a macrocosmic holographic projection of what is inside you"

"Our Universe is a fractal holographic projection of light, it is a mirror"

"There is no such thing as a straight line in our universe. All Light, Time/Space and Forces are curved, because they are all heading back to SOURCE and the CENTRAL POINT from which they manifested"

"At the centre of all things and each atom, is a divine spark. In everything from the microcosm to the macrocosm, our sun and stars are such things"

"Belief is a powerful force like gravity, and should be treated as such.

It is more important to understand WHY you believe something, than the actual belief itself"

"Every belief you cling to is a partial truth, a fraction of the whole. So how can any idea created through this Expression contain the whole truth? When our view is from but a fraction?"

"Forget all you know or think you know and hold no belief. Yet strive to be aware of all things and simply BE PRESENT within the moment. Know that you know nothing and nor does anyone."

"Be as water, able to hold all possibility yet not be limited in anyway. Water can mould into any form, break rock, yet be a single drop containing an ocean of infinite possibility. It is Pure because it carries no baggage."

"Do not limit your infinite possibility by belief, for it is this very thing that limits you in the first place and holds you prisoner to a partial truth. Restricting that which you have the potential to be."

"Subtle vibrational changes give rise to the wide variety of life manifest on this planet, in our universe and in the many dimensions"

"WE LIVE IN A WAVEFORM UNIVERSE, in a sea of motion. A Beautiful ocean of consciousness and symphony of life. Open your heart for Humans are antennas for waveforms."

"Gamma Rays are not a natural thing in our universe; they are created by Very Advanced Technology. They can bend space and time, for they are not restrained by the speed of light or the rules of this dimension. Many alien Races and beings have the ability to travel as A ULTRA HIGH FREQUENCY WAVEFORM. THE PHEONIX LIGHTS UFO SIGHTING was one prime EXAMPLE OF THIS"

"Everything is a mix of frequencies in this great symphony of life; we are all one unit of energy expressing itself"

"Thoughts and the power of emotion create reality. Thoughts create the Form and focal point, while emotion collapses the wave function of reality. Everything is consciousness"

"God created nature so we can always have a constant connection to our Higher Self"

*"I call that **the law of shining**, so if you shine what you want to be right now, the same as you shine out what you need in your life, it will come to you"*

"First learn what makes you happy and how to make yourself happy. Happiness is NOT A PURSUIT, it is a WAY OF BEING"

"You are the centre of your universe and the X point between all omnipresent worlds"

"Everything is vibrant conscious Living energy, when this energy gets isolated in a magnetic field this gives rise to all form and all being"

"All planets have life on them

on varying vibrational resonations"

"Everything is consciousness. After much time of repeating the same pre-set frequency loops again and again, energy in its isolated state, sometimes becomes Conscious onto itself. A being of the Creation itself is born that is not a creation of The Creator, Elementals are such beings"

"We are like a bubble. We exist within an illusionary isolated field of awareness, created by the power of magnetism."

"God The Creator creates infinitely and wastes no energy"

"All energy goes through the cycle of decline and descent, then it ascends and returns once more"

"In life all things that can arise, will arise.

If there is a possibility to do so"

"By fulfilling your part in God The Creators plan, it will draw unto thee, into alignment, and unto thy awareness. All those other beings who are also fulfilling their parts wholeheartedly, find them, work with them and nay deny them"

"There are tones and frequencies that can move mountains, for these vibrating frequencies of light in motion, are what create mountains in the first place"

"To have infinite complexity, start as simply as possible. All possibilities then exist and are thus are a living force to be brought into manifest form at any time"

"It is always darkest before the dawn, as the Void of Creation is opened for the new creation to be put into place. A space has been made, the track has finished, and a new song is about to play"

"The Universe is a Hall Of Mirrors to bounce light, all frequencies and harmonies of frequency occur around a single central point. This is but one purpose of Stars(Electro Magnetic Plasma Bubbles)"

"Sound vibrates around a central core / point / a singularity and builds form in this manner. We can now confirm that all planets are naturally created hollow. Our Moon is hollow, Mars is hollow, Earth is hollow, All planets are hollow, our Sun and all stars are also hollow, and contain within multiple dimensions"

"The bouncing off of these waveforms upon the central core (like waves upon a rock) give rise to the unique and individual tone and harmonic when the echo is perceived. When the frequencies of a harmonic hit one another (waves of expressive frequency/ vibration) this causes resistance. The resistance between interacting energy fields from our sun is what we feel as heat, and this resistance created by the magnetic field is also why we perceive our third dense light material dimension to be solid; when it is but an illusion to our human senses. This slowdown of ripple hitting ripple is what manifests time as we currently perceive it"

"All dimensions operate on harmonic scales/rates of vibration; the higher the frequency, the higher the complexity as the vibration increases, and the more the information can be transferred"

"The form Matter and Beings take, is entirely dependent upon its vibration"

"The Universe is but a reflection in a hall of mirrors, directly reflecting every thought, emotion, feeling and action. Your Focus becomes your reality"

"IN INFINITY everything you can imagine and are yet to imagine already exists somewhere in manifest form. Beings of every type exist in all forms and every harmonic variation. Every energetic pattern and frequency has its place in existence and is played out somewhere within all the dimensions.

Creatures are made of every element and of every size from the microcosm to the macrocosm, upon every level, creatures of all alignments of neutral, positive, and negative. There is no end to where life manifests and what expression it takes, all possibilities are played out in Gods symphony somewhere.

Where there is a possibility for life to manifest or a space, it will. For that is what Infinity is and what an infinite creator does, it CREATES INFINITELY"

"Consciousness is everything; there is nothing outside of consciousness. The mind is a tool for consciousness, it is not consciousness itself, for consciousness is non-local and hyper dimensional in nature"

"Reality is different depending upon who is looking at it, Creation tailors itself to the FOCAL POINT OF THE OBSERVER. The observer collapses the wave function of reality itself through the power of Thought, Emotion and PURE FOCUS"

"Satan = Mind / Ego / Body identification. Chosen disconnect from your Heart, Higher Self, Deeper Greater Mind, and Your True Identity of Oneness. It represents rebellion from Your True Unified True Self (the whole energy field)"

"The Human Mind is a reflective lens for the perceive world, it reflects everything backwards to reality, thus everything the Mind reflects is a lie. The Heart (Deeper Greater Mind) reflects everything truthfully as it is, for it is the LIVING TRUTH ITSELF"

"The Human Mind is not us, it creates a Self-identity and wants to be, but it is not. The ancients were well aware of this and called the mind 'the foreign installation' as those stuck in Mind live from a place of un-trueness"

"Good and Evil are man-made concepts, they are just extremes of the same energy, two components at war and never resolved. We must stick the concept back into one piece for its origin was born in Mind (untruth). The same must be done with all of our perceptions.

The lens filter of MIND splits consciousness into two reflections, one is light and the second is its shadow. Both perceptions although truly one, are what you perceive as good and evil. But they are truly one. Perceived evil originates from viewing the world through the lens/filter of Mind. As oppose to your true identity and Greater Deeper Mind of the heart, which exists in a state beyond good and evil"

"The more you feel disconnected from Your Central Point and True Greater Deeper Mind (True Identity), the worse the reflection of sickness, corruption and evil is reflected within the world, and the more darkness, confusion & chaos"

"The closer you are in True relationship with your Higher Self Connected to the Pure Energies of your Deeper Greater Mind, the more Harmonious and heaven like the experience - everything going in synch with no resistance in the energy flow. WE TRULY ARE BEINGS OF PURE ENERGY"

"When the will of man, follows the will of His Greater Deeper Mind, Higher Self, and True identity, the True UNION of HEART, MIND AND SOUL will occur"

"Animals do not see the world through their lens/ filter of Mind, so are without the chosen disconnect (Rebellion) from their true nature. They are in complete synch with the will of The Creator and of Mother Earth (The Creation). They do not take pleasure in killing one another, only man makes that choice"

"Killing, murder, war, and evil are not natural to man. They are all born in the Surface Shallow Human Mind when a false identity has been created, and the soul is lost in this desert of illusion. That is why people are traumatized in war, both victim and soldier alike. Some are traumatized consciously, while the truly evil ones unconsciously. As the fate they binded unto themselves through their action, haunt them forever as their future, even beyond this life. WAR IS A FORM OF HELL"

"Your True Form is the VIBRANT LIVING WELL of pure consciousness at the heart of your being. Separation from this is in but an illusion of Mind/Ego. We are one with all things, The WHOLE ENERGY FIELD is the TRUESELF. Live through your infinite HEART, Not your finite MIND, for it is the VOICE OF THE CREATOR and your TRUE POWER and identity is within, not outside"

"A person has TWO MINDS not just one and most cannot separate these aspects of themselves, and so end up following one of the many thousands of wrong voices. You have the human Mind that projects everything backwards to reality and projects its fears into the world and onto others, blaming them. Then you have the Deeper Greater Mind of the True self that sees everything as it is, it is stronger than the world and is unafraid"

"Thirst to want to know the truth of things even if you have to change everything about yourself, be unafraid"

"All evil arises when you give up POWER WITHIN to others outside, you must

TRUST YOUR OWN DIVINITY*"*

"The Soul is what fuels your consciousness and all life, reflecting your third dimensional image into this world. It is the place of peace you feel within. Think of the happiest you have been in your life, the great feeling of peace. Get to know that feeling for it is the frequency of your soul"

"Relax and surrender to your Higher Greater Self, Know your soul, know yourself"

"How can you discover the Light within, if you have belief and material possessions blocking you way and weighing you down?"

"Your natural state is one of pure energy, the place of peace you feel within, beyond all space and time. It is at the centre of your being and has many names. The Soul, Central Sun, Singularity, Zero Point.

Words are just an expression of energy, so it is only the meaning that is important and your understanding of what is being given. Raise your vibration by giving up all of the things that you do not need. Free your soul within and flow its unlimited potential into this world. Ascend by giving up all of the chains that keep you down."

"You are only limited to this third dimension if you think you are, for the limitation is in the thought itself and not what is or isn't possible. Consciousness is stronger than any wave of vibration created by other means. It's time to become Multidimensional once more. It's time to Unleash your inner potential into the world"

"You are a being of pure energy who's energy has been split into two parts and vibrational state lowered into matter. You must overcome this fractured state of consciousness and being to become a master of the third dimension, thus allowing you to open up back to your natural multidimensional state.

Because of this human conditional state, you have two minds, a Deeper True Mind of the Heart and a Surface Human Ego Mind. The heart must rule the Ego and be in True Relationship, to have peace, harmony and most importantly, **UNITY WITHIN**"

"You must understand that the human condition is like a coin, with two halves, two Minds. Never complete until they unite their two halves in True Relationship.

The Surface Shallow Human Ego (Personal Mind), serving the Hearts (Deeper Greater True Mind)"

"A human being has two minds, two beings, there's the True You and the human you ... and you need to put the two into a symbiotic relationship, their True Relationship"

"It's your Greater Deeper Mind you need to connect to and your Higher Self, which is not an individual it's a relationship, everything is relationship"

"Establish a relationship with your higher self and true mind daily. Transcend the ego by giving up the need to control people and the external world, wanting approval, validation, and judging others. The higher self, true you, stands tall on its own two feet without any of these egotist thought forms. It requires them not to know its own true self-identity and worth"

"The Ego is not the enemy, only when one surrenders unto the Ego or lets it control our every thought and action does it become a problem. The Ego is supposed to serve the Greater Deeper Higher True Mind within you, not rule you from moment to moment"

"Which ever part of yourself you feed the most, will become the dominant controlling force within your life"

"Only when you feed the Heart and Greater Deeper Mind more, will you have power over your Higher True Self and have the Ego in check and in true relationship"

"The Ego is the sleeping part of us that is yet to become fully aware of your Higher True Self. As a conduit of Self, through us it heals, through our light it awakens. So live through the heart and be love"

"You are flow, you are spirit, you are being-ness, you are awareness, and you are love"

"Enlightenment is not something you pursue; it is a state of being you just choose to be".

"Enlightenment is merely to make the choice to lighten oneself and have true relationship within. Allowing the Ego to serve the heart and not the heart serve the Ego"

"Hold and learn as much knowledge as you can, but hold none as belief to weigh you down"

"Enlightenment is to live only in awareness and experience, a lighter state of being, freeing you from all boundaries, burdens, and illusions"

"Bring as much of your True Higher Self into the world as you can daily, and it will refine you into what you already truly are"

"There is only one source for all life, the Mind likes to create thoughts about itself and create a Self. This is what births the Ego and that is the very part one must transcend to get back to their True Higher Self"

"The Creator assumes all forms, all forms are manifestations of the one. Although the Ego itself is a manifestation of the human mind created as a reflex to the environment"

"We are all one. So when we hear a truth, a bell goes off inside our hearts and resonates. We then know, YES that is true! Why? Because we are the truth itself, the whole energy field"

"The supreme truth is beyond the Mind and therefore beyond words and language; it expresses itself as words and language, but can never ever be fully described, **only felt**"

"The supreme ultimate truth exists in complete absence of itself, it is empty, it is nothingness, yet fullness"

"All DIVISION is Mind illusion"

"Capacity and concentration is power. The more unified a being and concentrated they are the more they will influence and effect the Minds of all beings around them, including the environment"

"A teacher is only a guide, to guide people into their own power. So they find their own heart, their own voice, and their own soul"

"Repeat, repeat, and repeat once more. Repetition is a shadow of concentration and thus bonds you to power. Become powerful through the experience of doing"

"POWER is bound to necessity"

"One of people's greatest mistakes in life is that they give power away. People are always looking for a saviour outside of themselves but the saviour dwells within."

"Never give power away to any man, alien, inter, hyper or pan dimensional being. There is already a hero inside each and every one of us, find your true heart,

FIND IT!"

"Those of faded faith and heart, living as shadows of their own potential in many areas of themselves, will easily be conquered. It is those of concentrated spirit, who do not walk as the shadow of their own enlightenment, who are redeemed and thus are a guiding light for the redemption of all. RECLAIM YOURSELF"

*"Do not think, **FEEL**.*

*Do not try, **DO**.*

*Do not move, **FLOW**.*

Do not waste time, for it is our most precious resource"

"You have two aspects existing simultaneously, the human aspect and your I AM PRESENCE. The full Vibrant living ocean super conscious Self. Many refer to it as Over soul, Central Sun, The Soul, Divine Spark, or Zero Point. Labels are not important, so you can simply call it HOME. For it is where we are all from and the place where consciousness is birthed (Luminous beings are we)"

"The human Soul which is hyper-dimensional in nature is living in what we perceive as paranormal circumstances on a daily basis. The soul splinters consciousness into many different parts. The totality of and True Real You is experiencing many different lives and in many forms, past, present and future alongside your existence here simultaneously. For there is only one now moment and all time is simultaneous.

However always remember that this is the life that is the most important for it is where you are right now, and where you have your point/anchor of awareness attached to in space and time. Knowing too much when one does not have the capacity for it, can make you go crazy. So Focus only upon your life in this world and what you are PRESENTLY DOING for that is what is truly important.

With this knowledge simply, be at peace in knowing you are far greater than just a Human Being and the journey is far, far longer plus more beautiful than anyone could ever possibly imagine"

"Remove as much MIND out of ones activities as one can. Remove as much MIND from all aspects of one's life as one can. The more MIND, the more distortion in you on all levels. Step out of the way of Gods awakening for you. Flow your HIGHER SELF into the world through True Relationship and Align with your DEEPER GREATER MIND"

"Evol u ti on = Love, U No It

LOVE IS EVOLUTION"

"**We become what we do**.

The choice of evolution is always ours."

"It is not outside learning that brings about evolution of mind body and spirit. But the EXPERIENCE OF DOING"

'What you gain through experience can never be taken away from you, it becomes a part of you, and that's true evolution'

"When it comes to THE QUESTION OF EVOLUTION, regardless of what others are doing or the state of the worlds, do not let them slow you down, derail you, or bring you down to their level.

Do not resist their creation, simply focus everything you have, your full resources and full integrity on what you are creating moment to moment – your creation, your community.

Let your Deeper Greater Mind lead yourself onto THE GOLDEN PATH OF DIVINE EVOLUTION. The path you take is always in your hands"

'In the reclamation of Knowledge there is no limit to the vastness and wonderment of what can be received, once you reach that place of evolved reception that allows it to flow. Then the revelations will flow like a waterfall into river, cascading down and through you in a rhythmic dance of love and expansion'

"Knowledge is power,

but ONLY WHEN APPLIED"

"Wisdom is Evolution as applied"

"Patience is but one stepping stone to wisdom"

"Patience is nourishment for the soul and patience is also a KEY of teaching"

"Own your fears, your sorrow, and your pain. It is yours and belongs to you"

"Sitting at the bottom of hell, we are afraid of our own immortality, it fears me not"

"Titans must occupy the space less trod"

"FOCUS, with intent of the highest good"

"Intelligence in the universe is how you adapt to change quickly, so if you want to become intelligent then just become adaptive, become fluid – be as water"

"Through the experience of integration, that's when you evolve, that's evolution, that's what makes you powerful"

"Everything can be known within stillness as it connects you to absolutely everything, because you completely take you, the small you, out of the equation"

"As soon as you take the 'I' out of the equation, the small you, it allows the Greater You to emerge"

"Truth is not something you just become aware of and that's it, it's a long refining process to refine you from one state of being to another one, it can't just flick on. You can have awakenings where you feel like a light is switched on, and you can change consciousness and create those anchor points. But there is a slow process to get you from where you were to where you are now, and where you are going, even when you do have epiphanies"

"You don't even need to get to the goal of where you are going, so long as you have a goal and a general direction, that's a good thing"

"People have an idealistic view of how they want things to turn out and that basically invites disappointment...the True Self is just happy if you are going in the right direction and becoming closer to who you truly are"

"This is no time for revolution, as the establishment all through our history are the ones who benefit. Revolutions come around and around binding humanity in circles and chains; it is time for EVOLUTION, for that lasts for all time.

That state is a constant one does not come back from. So let us evolve and to evolve, take action daily right now, because we become what we do. There is no time like the PRESENT!"

"When I say everything is one I always remind myself that on the highest level there is no difference between me and anybody else. We all have the same potential, the same power, we just need to remember how to use it"

"I wanted to know the truth no matter what that meant for me, or my ideas, or myself, no matter what I thought of myself, or others, or the world. Then I found that the truth is already alive and well inside yourself, and anything outside is just to enrich your inner truth"

"When you give to others and give to something greater than yourself you are expanding more into your potential, you're expanding more into your True Self"

"If you do self-work and you're strong in yourself, it's going to make everyone else stronger as well"

"If you do stillness every day, meditation, then you'll be more sensitive to everything, to people who are true and people who are not. You'll have a gut feeling – it's called communion with Your Higher True Self"

"Meditation is LISTENING TO GOD,

Prayer in its expression is talking to God"

"Everyone around you is a reflection, and the universe, and people are teachers, you just need to put yourself in a space where you are learning"

"You need to find out what your nature is and go in that direction, and it will feel very peaceful for you. The more you're following your TRUE PURPOSE and DESTINY the more peace you are going to feel"

"True spirituality will always make you stronger. It will take you out of the world for small amounts of time but it will always bring you back to the world armed to the teeth with spiritual knowledge and ready to serve God The Creator"

"Everything has a purpose so you need to realise what the purpose is, and anything you learn you need to bring back into the world and give it to others, give it to the world because that's what it's really for. It's not even about us; it's about giving what we have to create a better world, to improve it"

"You must have a relationship with your Higher Self, it's not an individual it's a relationship… then you can't be put in any box ever, because you're greater than the people trying to put you in a box. You're far more aware, far more focused, and because of that you're far more concentrated, and concentration is power in a Being"

"Let me now make it clear what the FALLEN ANGELS ARE. They represent the REBELLION VS SELF. Every angel archetype represent THE ENEGIES WITHIN OURSELVES.

These energies can be used for GREAT GOOD or great evil.

When living in EGO and not the heart we are the fallen angels, accept we did not fall, we are not imprisoned. We chose to be here on a journey to full self-awareness in this AGE OF EGO.

The angels were never supposed to be seen as an outside enemy or force greater than yourself, but be used to understand the potential energies WITHIN OURSELVES"

"What is Mighty and fearsome is powerless to effect a mighty and fearless man"

*"The priesthoods of every age and every continent have always been hostile to freedom. The Shadow governments have taken the **REGRESSIVE PATH OF INVOLUTION**"*

"Knowing is of the Mind (illusion), awareness is of the INIFINITE HEART (full potential and open to all possibilities).

Let your INFINITE HEART and not your Finite Mind be the eyes you use to perceive. It has infinite potential unlike the Mind, so is true to The Law of Unity and Oneness"

"True wisdom starts when you are aware that, You truly know nothing"

"All of this only exists so you can become more self-aware. It is paramount that you create a SINGULAR TRUTH within, in all you do, think or perceive. BE the EMBODIMENT OF TRUTH AND LIGHT. A beacon for the world. Dissolve all inner barriers into Oneness and be whole, or as Plato says, a circle"

"LIVE HEART.

Limited finite perceptions and potential, viewing the world through your Mind and not the heart is what those who seek control over you want. When they get you to identify with the body and Mind, you limit your full potential. Your True identity is already established within before you were born, it is not something that is given to you. When you think of yourself as the body and not one with the whole of creation, this is where the JOURNEY OF UNTRUTH into the DESERT OF ILLUSION starts"

"Make all of your perceptions abstract and not a part of you, perceive with HEART not MIND. If you hold a belief other than that of your own infinite potential and that of others, this is a downward path to implosion"

"Belief is a limited created temporal structure within your energy field that limits you and all of your projections and perceptions. Unless you make your belief infinite and true to the LAW OF UNITY AND ONENESS. (Everything is whole / one).

When people hold belief, this temporal construct becomes a part of their body, because they have made it a part of themselves. When you try to help them and open them up beyond their belief, they see it as an attack upon themselves and their body, because they have already made the mistake of identifying themselves with it. They see their belief as truth, when it is but an objective and abstract way of understanding reality.

This is what is Wrong with religion, people make their beliefs part of themselves instead of like all concept's A MEANS TO

UNDERSTAND. They then unify into a stronger force to enforce this distortion on others as the only way. This distortion is an ILLNESS THEY GAINED through lack of SELF RESPONSIBILITY of being A CREATOR"

"The Self Proclaimed Elite, the priesthood's and all of their allies, want POWER OUTSIDE THEMSELVES to fill THE VOID OF INSECURITY within themselves. They are the most afraid out of anybody, they contain the MOST FEAR WITHIN.

Because they FEEL Disconnected from what they truly are, they LACK AWARENESS OF SELF. Operating from Mind, Ego, their own Shadow, and from their own Inner Demons. The spiritual war on Terra wages.

Any beings who rebel against God and who have been over taken by their own Shadow, and fear inside themselves, do not create their own energy. Because they have disconnected themselves from their SOURCE OF INFINITE POTENTIAL (Well of Life). They use you to provide them with energy, you are used to sustain them and *their rebellion. The pyramid of control on this world is not set up to enslave you (that would cost too much energy).*

It is set up so YOU ENSLAVE YOURSELF WILFULLY (without you even being consciously aware), and it limits you IMPORTANT INFORMATION TO LIMIT YOUR PERCEPTION OF REALITY AND OF YOUR SELF. Ask yourself one important question. Which way is the energy flowing in your life? It is a world of Vampires and Magicians"

"Cut yourself off from all outside ties to the system, be sovereign and let no one vampire your creational energies"

'Fear is just a guide, an ally, to show you what you have to integrate and overcome to get back home to your True Self'

"No matter how powerful or omnipresent a shadow, a monster, or an enemy may seem. Once it dissolves from memory and is forgotten, it ceases to hold power"

"One family,

One Love"

"Show a Human the way to land and they will go live there and never be content nor fulfilled. Show the Human Being how to find land by itself and it will find its TRUE HOME"

"God The Creator of all things, never forces things on any being on any level, change is good but only if you allow it to unfold naturally"

"When you are writing, you are not writing in a language, but as a language"

"The only power another being has, is the power you give up within yourself"

"You must Learn to create great effects within the Universe, yet remain Small & unseen, for the Wise must remain hidden"

"You must understand RELIGION and SPIRITUALITY are 100% incompatible. Why is this? Because Religion (External) is about conquering and controlling an individual, and the other, Spirituality, (Internal) is about the personal growth and personal development of an individual.

YOU ARE MULTIDIMENSIONAL,

THINK THAT WAY!"

"Only the pure of heart, have the power to resist the allure of corruption from the selfish mind"

"Only courageous action within this world and universe has a future. Only courageous acceptance of the challenge creates the free race of man"

"Nothing man puts his mind to is out of his reach, in the united human family"

"One small group of highly focused people can help change the world and even one person can directly affect the destiny of the entire universe"

"If you do not learn from the past you bind yourself to it and will be doomed to repeat it once again, it will present itself in your future as fate"

"I give up space within and unbind that which is no longer serving me, to create space for my dreams and destiny"

"Oppose all deception and be pure of heart"

"The quieter one becomes,

the more one can hear"

"The Earth is a living conscious being, an organism with veins, capillaries, arteries and a Heart"

"Earth is a living conscious being like us, and is part of us. The Earth can live without man, but man cannot live without The Earth"

"The Sun and Earth are powerful Conscious Beings of Abundance; they give & give & give. Without their constant giving, we could not exist"

"Everything is Consciousness, thus EVERYTHING has a **secret lesson within** itself that you can learn, if you look closely and deeply at its magic within"

"Once awareness expands, it never goes back nor returns to its original size or dimension. Concentration is POWER, when these new expansions of awareness are brought back to oneself"

"All our thoughts and actions come from our soul. All our experiences, fears, pain, hurt, pleasant moments, moments of happiness, love, kindness, compassion, faith, dreams, hope, laughter, and tears. They all represent little pieces of our soul. We are always looking for a soul mate and those who will aid us in our greater works, we are being pulled towards our true relationships. Sometimes consciously and for most people unconsciously. Each person has a soul mate and spiritual family. The real question is have you left enough room in your life for your true relationships, for your destiny?"

"Those connected to their True Higher Self are never alone, The Greater Soul is never alone, indeed it is true"

"In a very turbulent and chaotic environment, what you need is stability... that stability comes from within yourself"

"That's what makes a powerful spiritual person, they are not affected as much, they go through bad stuff but it makes them stronger. They take it as learning experience, learning curve, and know it's to serve them, ultimately making them more powerful. And life strengthens you, thats why we are here"

"If you want to become a highly conscious aware being, then start living that life now. Then already you've succeeded, because from that point on, you are already living as a highly conscious Human Being, and you will create ripples"

*"If you give everything

you will get everything"*

"When people come into this world they have a cargo, like a gift they have to deliver into the world, so you have to find what that is and give it to others and the world"

"Standing Rock is prophecy in motion, it is the dawning and sunrise of earths greatest ever tribe, The Tribe of The Human Being. The tribe who possesses and brings forth the rainbow, the rainbow of liquid light that heals all things and brings forth the unification of the human family"

"The Rainbow Tribe consisting of every nation, creed, and colour upon this world of Terra Nova (Earth) is Humanity's True path. It is the LIGHT to the darkness and shadow of the emerging Fourth Reich."

"A storm is coming, be prepared. Always have Faith an Hope. Know THYSELF. For Great Darkness always comes before the Greatest Dawn. The rewards and gifts of what comes after when the darkness is dissolved will be a direct reflection of the amount of darkness endured in the struggle."

"Honour to the ancestors and children yet to come"

"If we try to carry to much weight, we become prisoners to our own creations, so one must learn when to let go, let them be free and have a life of their own"

"Address the universe with integrity and the future belongs to you. The future belongs to those who believe in the beauty of their dreams"

*"Any being or object that is vibrating faster than us, will **appear as light** to us from our third dimensional perspective"*

"Upon every dimensional frequency harmonic is another version of you, living simultaneously and omni-presently in a reality alongside you. Take control of your True Self, the Divine Spark at your core and you will gain the ability to project a part of your energy into any world or reality anywhere and in any time, for you are no longer thinking in limited linear terms.

When you can leave your human form upon command on some level and you have knowledge of your True Self, then you have truly awoken to your True SELF and multidimensional Legacy. To be able to do this is a NATURAL THING, to not remember it is UNNATURAL.

The Ancients knew about it and used it, it was common knowledge among their people. Open your heart and cultivate a Singular truth within"

"The God Head divides and splits into multiple parts to produce a reflection of itself like a hologram. On Each dimensional harmonic is another part of your I AM PRESENCE existing simultaneously."

"Consciousness builds in layers, in steps one above the other, just like a Mayan pyramid. Without the lower blocks of consciousness in place, this dimension and human experience could not exist as it currently and presently is"

"All dimensions above our dimension or that have come before have access to all of the informational content of the dimension below. What this means is, just because a being knows all information about you and your mind, plus its thoughts, and exactly where you are in perceived space-time, it does not make them a God nor does it make them good"

"Reptilian Consciousness and Beast Consciousness existed upon the earth before the concept of Man had even been invented or Domain of Man birthed into being. These Lower levels of consciousness are a part of your human design. Weather you accept it or not, but it does not mean you have to become them"

"Man has Reptilian qualities and Beast Consciousness qualities as a part of their lower consciousness, because this dimensional construct/reality is BUILT UPON the consciousness of being that came before this moment in Time. Hence our Reptilian brain"

"Some people in our world operate though the lower levels of their consciousness, They are afraid of man being what he truly already is, INFINITE LOVE"

"Man has the ability to build reality and create it as he sees fit, man's thoughts shape reality from moment to moment and create new shifts in relation to this ultimate truth. This is happening now whether you realize it consciously or unconsciously"

"A Language which is set within a fixed form is stagnant, it is a dead language. A language must be fluid, it must be ever changing and evolving to be alive. If the language does not have the words required, invent new ones. For it is the essence, meaning, and deeper communication of words that is important, not the form of the word or structure itself"

"Your choice of Conscious Expansion is in EACH MOMENT, and will be reflected in the Universe by granting you awareness through Direct Personal Spiritual Experiences"

"The Universe is a PORTAL FOR THE SOUL"

"BECOME an aspect of your I AM PRESENCE within the world itself.

Become one with the ETERNAL NOW"

"Align you Human Self with your Greater Deeper Mind and TRUE INNER DIVINE SELF, the universe will then be your ally. BE THE LIVING TRUTH in each moment and the same equal reflection will be granted back. To be aware of truth is TO BE TRUTH or be on that path. Good journey"

"The lower aspects of Man's Consciousness tries to dominate the higher aspects, do not allow the lower aspects of your own consciousness to become the Driving/Dominant force in your life. Thus trapping you in illusions of Your Human Personal Mind"

"Do not allow your Human Personal Mind to convince you to look outside of yourself for truth, do not allow it to convince you that you are weak and have no power. The Spiritual war on consciousness is the war we face within our world. To be 100% within your own POWER in each moment, is too focus upon that which you wish TOO CREATE as opposed to that which you resist.

Simply Be ON ALL LEVELS RESPONSIBLE, do not look outside yourself for truth. Do not give power away and then you are beyond any form of being able to be deceived or controlled"

"The Human Personal Mind is known as the foreign installation, this is where the Father of Lies and Ego Consciousness is birthed forth from, the Mind reflects things backwards to reality. The heart always tells the truth, for it is the whole energy field and represents your Deeper Greater Mind and Voice of Your True Divine Self. LEARN TO TELL THE DIFFERENCE"

"Align with Your Infinite Heart and not the Finite Mind, Become the **I AM**

of each divine moment"

"Personal attachment cuts you off from UNIVERSAL KNOWLEDGE, you must have an objective mind to gain true knowledge"

"We have all cultivated the idea of a subjective self, giving ourselves a false identity from birth. THAT is what all MIND PROJECTIONS such as cultural media, social networking, advertising and body identification are all about. But if you do not believe or conceive of your own divinity, how are you going to leap into the next levels of evolution and magnetize true unconditional Love and respect onto yourself without thinking in this way? Thus change yourself individually and collectively we will change the world together and build the vision we hold within"

"If no power is given away to outside influence and full responsibility is accepted, you have not created a VOID BLACK SPACE within, that EXTERNAL forces will try to fill. The governments and institution's that prey upon your energy, will never manifest into third dimensional experience"

"One of mankind's biggest problems is Mankind is taking truths personally, filtering it through there Ego and Mind. Instead of through their Hearts Greater Deeper Mind and seeing it as an objective truth for reality. All religions, dogma's and beliefs systems within this world are distortions of this mistake"

"The problems of our world are not external ones, they are **INTERNAL.**

The world is a direct reflection.

This war is a SPIRITUAL one,

not a physical one "

"Mankind fell asleep and it appears he had help to do so. A lot of mankind has been put on the path of materialistic power, fake immortality, or the path of technology. Any path that creates separation from its TRUE SELF and Inner divine self"

"There is more proof that ET is here and also out there than they are not. Those Dark Forces who are in power do not want you to know the truth of life in the Universe, they do not want you to know who YOU ARE because once you do their game is all but over"

"The First empires to take control in Our Universe, were not worldly or galactic in nature, But interdimensional"

INTERDIMENSIONAL

V V V V

GALACTIC

V V V V

WORLDLY

"Our technology is a direct reflection of ourselves and our own consciousness level, if we want to change anything within our world, we first must change ourselves.

Responsibility is the KEY to the world you want to SEE"

"There is an alien intervention operating within the world, not in the best interests of the human family"

"The main question about the UFO phenomenon that should be asked is not, are these objects real? Where do they come from? Or who/what is flying them? But what do these manifestations tell us about ourselves? What do we need to learn about ourselves in order that we should have the manifest experience in the first place? For they are but a reflection, and nothing can be fully understood by the very essence of itself"

"Life exists on every frequency and in every place known, and unknown. It is a universal manifestation"

"Most of the living universe is unseen to us, we just need the right tools to be able to see it"

"Most life in our universe operates out of the frequency range and the ranges of the human five senses"

"There is a vast panorama of life, including intelligent life in our universe that is veiled from normal human sight"

"We need to create devices and apparatus ourselves that will remove all our optical limitations in our seeking of life around us and within the universe"

"Our entire existence, environment, and living scenario is completely conditioned by domains we cannot see directly.

The same thing applies at the lower end of nature (microcosmic) and the upper end of nature (macrocosmic)"

"There are many forms of Light, use them all when searching for life in this living conscious universe"

"Most UFO's that operate within our world cannot be seen with the naked eye, you must use infrared, ultra violet, night vision, all available spectrums and concave lenses to detect them"

"When searching for life in this universe be imaginative and use every means necessary"

"Time to go hunting for life on all spectrums and frequency bands"

"Everyone forgets that life not only exists in the micro world, but in the macro world as well"

"Life is adapted for survival in every place accepted and currently unaccepted. It is a universal manifestation"

"Life Exists on all levels of creation, space crawls with life. We are surrounded by life"

"Dark matter in our universe is just the omnipresent realities we are unable to decode and perceive in our current human condition, for our human five senses only see a very small spectrum of light and are very limited"

"Different beings reside in all the many spectrums of light and darkness. These Demons and Angels exist beyond the dimensions of space, time, and Mind"

"We are the projector of light, we are the X point between all light and dark. The X point (You) is a very important intersection of light and dark, it is a gate that gives birth to all images."

"Some beings will try to influence your thoughts and will try to manipulate you in what we call the Mental Environment, for they exist in the light and dark beyond the base of Mind. Always wear your spiritual armour"

"We are a gateway between all worlds, we are the mirror"

"The Matrix we are in exists so we can become fully aware of projections of Self, both aspects good and bad"

"You are Creators born in the image of the One Creator, CREATION is your God given power, utilize it fully. CREATE the environment for your reality to emerge."

"And that is how it always starts when something births into life and first comes into being, it is very small, it is hardly noticed. When did that moment begin? When did it happen? Yet the consequences of it will be felt by all, for years, decades, even hundreds of years later, perhaps millions, billions or more."

"Let a complex system play itself out indefinitely and eventually something remarkable and surprising is bound to occur"

"There is good out there but they are not going to come down here and clean up our mess. Because if they did we would not be strong enough to survive beyond our world, and from that moment forth we would be dependent upon them and locked together in time. We must deal with what we create (Our Own Projections), it is our responsibility. Individually and then together collectively we must RISE TO THE OCCASION."

"UFO's, Alien Beings, and inter-dimensional beings can serve as a reminder for us and a catalyst to realize THE TRUTH WITHIN OURSELVES, but Our True Allies do not interfere, nor would they. There are no benevolent races out there that would interfere in human affairs. We must cultivate our own energy within, develop a relationship with our Higher True Self daily and cultivate a Powerful Singular Truth within.

Because we are one and everything is connected, all parts are equal, THE SAVIOUR IS ALIVE & WELL WITHIN YOU."

"Do not expect a saviour from outside oneself and you will not be open up to deception"

"With great power and mastery over oneself comes much responsibility, we must each seek the Divine Creator Spark within ourselves individually, before we can build the future of our dreams that we wish to create. By reconnecting with our true identity within, we are given infinite power over oneself and the universe itself becomes an ally.

This means we can face any challenge that arises at any time and in any place or in any moment. Master yourself to a high degree and your will master the world to a high degree"

"The flood myths from The Bible and all over The Earth from every single continent have been proven true, but our true history is not taught or propagated"

"There was a great flood and the ancients were all but destroyed"

"Most of our human history is below the oceans and in the places you least expect"

"The Great Flood, that of ancient times which sunk a whole civilization, can easily be proven"

"The ancients, hunted they were and forced underground"

"The very Wise must stay hidden to survive within this universe"

"Mankind has been around a very, very long time. An ancient people are we"

"The ancients domination was worldly it stretched the globe, but even more than that, beyond this world. It is very clear with 100% certainty to those of true heart, and the powerful spark of Creator Soul, that Human kind is **living within the ruins of what we once were**"

"We are the remnants of this Ancient Advanced Earth Stretching Civilization"

"When it comes to the highly advanced scientific civilization of The Ancients, perceived mythology once again just transmuted into LIVING REALITY"

"The ancients were trying to mirror the stars above on the ground below, many of the ancient structures all over this world and beyond are a lot older than the 5000 years admitted. Many are aligned with stars 10,000 to 17,000 Years ago. They all come from a common source, the all but lost and destroyed civilization of The Ancients, now re-emerging back into Human Consciousness and remembrance"

"It is with great certainty and is quite apparent that a world-wide stretching civilization was wiped out in the great flood, one much older and ancient than mainstream history wishes to show"

"Our true human origins have been hidden for the empowerment of the few over the masses, this war and disempowerment agenda of the few. Over the origins of the human race, continues just as strong today. For he who controls the past, can shape the future"

"On the bottom of the seas lies all of the once proud cities"

"Your past is your future and your future is your past"

"When the ancients were drawing submarines, helicopters and other the transportation devices, they were showing that which was destroyed BEFORE THE GREAT FLOOD. They were drawing their Future, YOUR PAST"

"YOU ARE NOT THIS, you are a prehistoric people and those who took the advancements and true knowledge of what went on that time have advanced further than you could know to be. Many of the craft that you see in the universe and in your sky, I tell you your own people are there. For they have the knowledge of this time and are advanced, while keeping you locked in the darkness of the past. THEY ADVANCE TO THE FUTURE, keeping you a slave race, YOUR EYES HAVE BEEN SHIELDED FROM SEEING THE TRUTH"

"In this world, and within the greater community of worlds, one of the most effective ways to suppress a nation or group of people is to put a device in place that will disassociate those people from their God, spirituality, and history. So a device was put in place that would ensure the perpetual empowerment over the minds of the people whom they deceived"

"Almost all left over knowledge from the truth of the last cycle was sequestered by the few self-proclaimed elites for their own empowerment"

"And there were GREAT WARS BACK THEN, that have been completely erased FROM THE MINDS OF MAN"

"The first real world war started not in the early 20th century as is told in western civilization, but when the American Indian nations were genocided by the hidden architects of this world"

"ALL KNOWLEDGE within this world is divided into two groups. Exoteric knowledge is taught to all people everywhere in all countries, through institutions, such as schools, universities and colleges, whilst ESOTERIC knowledge is hidden from the masses and taught only to initiated members of brotherhoods and secret societies ruling from the shadows. As has always been here on Earth, since the fall of The Ancients. The saying KNOWLEDGE IS POWER dates from this ancient lost world"

*"A civilization in ruins,

an Age Forgot"*

"Long ago in the far distant past was a beautiful wondrous civilization that misused the KEYS OF HIGHER KNOWLEDGE. They abused that knowledge and were unable to save themselves from the last great human cataclysm, thus they lost the keys and all of their higher knowledge"

"The same forces that have been greatly responsible for the GREAT DECEPTION AND DESTRUCTION OF MANKIND in ancient times, THE SHETU, Those who Seize, Abduct and Reprogram. A Predator / Parasitic Force, Have always been and still are the SHADOW GOVERNMENT within this world. These beings still remain the dominant force within our world behind the curtain."

"Every time the Human Race unlocks the SECRETS OF THE UNIVERSE AND OF THE SOUL, creates unity, stability, a good life for all of its people and COMPLETE PEACE, it falls prey to the greed of the ruling hierarchies and the power that was gifted onto these spiritually hollow creatures. Mankind then slips into chaos, war, and the Great Abyss of Darkness that brings great destruction that traumatizes the species once more. This is by no means a coincidence or an accident. The SHETU are the hidden agents, the hidden hand and the true instigators of this Darkness."

"Those Dark Forces in power do not want you thinking in multi-dimensions, but want you to stay in a SELF CONTAINED BOX of ignorance, assumption, and false beliefs."

"The human race will never be free, until it deals with The Shadow at the heart of itself"

"Our history as I have shown is far older and greater than has ever been taught, and this is not the first time as a race that we have reached this level of technology"

"The evil of past ages still lingers, the fragments of consciousness that refuses to move on"

"DNA is a shimmering wave form configuration that can be modified by light, radiation, sonic pulses, or magnetic fields. The harmonic science of The Ancients can affect DNA itself as well as all matter. It was a civilization that had cracked the genetic codes of all life including human life, they could re-programme it and bend it to their own will. They possessed the keys of the physical spectrum and knew the blueprint for the entire matrix of reality itself"

"ENOCH means **TO SPEAK**, to invoke, or enact.

EVERY POINT in space and time has a specific frequency signature that is unique.

The KEYS the ancients possessed turn out to be sound keys, keys to the vibratory Matrix of reality itself "

"All main pyramids are placed with Great Purpose; pyramids are microcosmically placed to produce stellar spin macrocosmically"

"The ancients were masters of sound and time. Capable of directly effecting the nervous system of all living systems and could produce profound effects of healing. They could easily induce higher states of consciousness and bring down the thin magnetic wall of energy that separates all omnipresent worlds"

"Language of Light, Language of Perfection, Language of Transcendence, Language of God The CREATOR. This beautiful spiritual science of the Highest Order and language describes a genetic stairway to the stars themselves"

"Our true history is infinitely more complex than anything ever taught. All ancient mythologies, legends, stories, and epics within our world, and upon every continent, have plenty to say about our history more than 12,000 Years ago. Despite what is said in mainstream history taught within institutions.

The whole of our human history has been fabricated and re- written. The true Human story spans many worlds and has a trail back to distant stars and a destiny that is among them too"

"The earth is a motor. The ancients knew this well and created natural structures from natural materials to plug into the Earth. They could tap unlimited energy from this, because they understood we live in a sea of motion. The ancients constructed a worldwide stretching antenna array that sat upon The Earth Grid. These pyramids were not only placed upon our world but also upon other bodies within our solar system. They were employed by ancient priest scientists as a musical system, amplifying the hyper-dimensional energies of The Multiverse, they acted as weights stabilizing the Earth's energy field becoming too chaotic (so pole shift does not occur as violently again) like in ages passed.

Cutting through all omnipresent realities and worlds, they act as star gates, between all dimensions of earth, both inner and outer"

"Every single star system is mapped upon the earth's surface and upon the planetary bodies around us, because to gain access to this star system/world one must have the symbol for the star system and use the star gates to project through. The VERY STARS Themselves are a language ENDCODED INTO OUR VERY OWN DNA and then reflected outwards macrocosmically. You truly are a Multidimensional Being and live within A Hologram Matrix of The Divine!"

"Pyramids and certain KEY EARTH GRID LOCATIONS are doorways between all omnipresent dimensions, and amplify the natural human ability to reach these dimensions contained within ourselves. The Ancients knew this well and it was common knowledge among their people"

"The Universe is a Conscious Living Being and we are experiencing ourselves subjectively"

*"**Vibration is the KEY to the Multiverse,** both in terms of the microcosm and macrocosm. Vibration is a KEY that SETS YOU FREE"*

"The land mass upon the earth, how high and where it is placed is a direct reflection of the consciousness level and the vibrations of the populations upon its surface. If the human race is not left to be free and express itself properly, if DNA is not set free, the fate of Atlantis will be blinded to its future"

"The populations of Atlantis were suppressed, that is why the earth shook and it sank into the depths in a single night and day of misfortune. It was no mystery, DNA must be set free"

"The Ancients had the technology not only to create vast amounts of energy from matter, they could also create matter itself from energy. A feat our current human civilization is yet to duplicate"

"The Ancients understood EVERYTHING IS ONE. They had technology that could merge energy fields, they could take any two objects and merge them into ONE. To be able to meld two seemingly different objects or more into one object, is NOT DEMONIC nor is it MAGIC, it is TECHNOLOGY"

*"When two beings are melded into one conscious being it is known as an **ARCHON**"*

"And there EXIST the **Ourobori** (Ouroboros), the oldest most ancient creatures who dwell upon the earth. They Emit Light, Contain Beings within themselves, and are within an orb form. Some of these OuroBori contain a whole collective consciousness within their orb form and reflect hundreds of faces in a single orb. However, these creatures aside, there are many types of orbs. They are a means for a being to project themselves or a part of their consciousness into omnipresent worlds, realities and dimensions. But Perhaps the Ourobori are doing just that already?"

"Some beings wilfully resist against the creator itself, trying to stay immortal and playing their own game, while slowly and surely, losing the connection to their Divine Eternal True Self"

"There exists beings from the ancient worlds, fragments of consciousness that refuse to move on. Twisted and tormented souls, convoluted in consciousness through their own discord. These Beings represent the True Rebellion against God, they wage war upon creation itself, but do not have the power to replicate it. God is PERFECT, all God's creatures are imperfect in their creations"

"These Beings, A Dark Predatory Parasitic Force, Self Proclaimed Pan Dimensional Gods. Sing out of tune with Gods symphony, their notes and tones are in rebellion to the harmony of God The Creator. They try to corrupt what is in God's creation. They twist things, perverting and corrupting as they go. Free will created the space/possibility to allow the Origin of Evil to emerge."

"Being a Living conscious Being, the Earths Destiny is to ascend. When the earth moves closer to the creator, those consciousness aspects who resist the creator's benevolence, who use fear as a weapon, and who create karma for themselves, are left behind. Thus the BEINGS and fragments of consciousness from ages passed before ours and who resisted, who created too much dense energy and karma for themselves, are some of the beings who are trying to beguile the human race now"

"All those beings who try to control and dominate through fear will be stuck here as we transcend the third dimension of perceived human experience"

"When people are desperate and in a state of fear, living within the lower aspects of their consciousness, in a state of wanting to be saved, the Dark Forces will always present the solutions to the problems that they created in the first place. Your Inner Divine Self will protect you from this, because it does not REACT, it RESPONDS"

"Any being who wilfully resists the creators benevolence, then who chooses to harm other beings wilfully upon any level, can be classed as a Fallen Angel"

"Do not fall for the ultimate deception of our time, do you really think the dark will come as such? THEY WILL COME as friends surrounded by LIGHT, otherwise people will not accept them. They will come offering you solution at the right pre-planned time of chaos"

"Canst thou love purely enough to bond thy Sweet Mysterious Destrious energies of the Pleiades, whilst break the cold, dark, Ancient binds of Orion?"

"Evil has a beginning, a middle, and an end. With **one final chord** of the highest order at the eschaton, piecing the firmament and into the darkest depths of all perceived hells. God because it is Far Greater & ANYTHING IS POSSIBLE FOR GOD, in its Great Mastery, resolves it all. "

"Heaven and hell is but a state of being and mind, both heaven and hell are within"

"Bear all you can, when you can, but be mindful of the BALANCE OF ALL THINGS"

"Say nothing and do nothing beyond what you know, but what you know. Make sure to apply, share and gift it unto the world"

"If we can understand the place we exist within right now, without letting it freak us out, if we can just face it, then we stay in Our POWER.

It's all a drama, it's all about creating war, it's all about distracting us and creating a space of fear. Because if we are in a space of fear, then we are not creating within a space of LOVE.

When we are in fear we basically imprison ourselves and put ourselves in a box. When we're not in fear we are FREE TO CREATE. In fear they are in control, in love, WE ARE IN CONTROL. That's all IT IS."

"It's the same drama that's been playing itself out for thousands of years. It's the kind of renaissance in human

consciousness, occurring very slowly before and rapidly now. It is not religious in nature but spiritual (Spiritual = The Full Totality of Truth and all of space time, seen and unseen). We are rediscovering something about human life on this planet, about what our existence means. This knowledge will alter human culture dramatically.

We're beginning to glimpse an alternative kind of experience, moments in our lives. We are sensing again, as in childhood, that there is another side to life that we are yet to rediscover. Some other process operating from behind the scenes.

Individuals have been aware of these unexplained coincidences throughout history. But the difference now lies in the numbers. The transformation is occurring now because of the number of individuals having this awareness, at the same time. And the number of people who are conscious of such coincidences are rapidly growing, and when a significant number of individuals seriously question what's going in life, we will begin to find out.

Other insights will be revealed, one after the other. All in reflection and in direct relationship to human consciousness.

THE FUTURE IS NOW!"

"I stay PRESENT to life right now. Right now this moment. No past, or future. THAT is where I always am mostly now. It takes a big burden off any worries. Every thought is like baggage that piles up and makes you un-stabilised.

Meditation is great because you cut all your bags and throw them in the sea, so to speak. Just you, PRESENT right now, no thoughts/mind, you already have everything you need, as do we all, we can CREATE Anything"

"The only constant in the universe IS CHANGE, when you come to peace with that then you will feel relaxed. I'm constantly changing hour by hour, day by day :-). I understand well. I do the same things but always becoming more refined and powerful on each vortex spin into the infinite. My life, I follow the greater plan so my mind does not create it. I listen to what my Deeper Mind wants.

Go do what you know you need and should do. THAT also brings GREAT PEACE. I need stillness at certain levels or I can't operate, and I shut down to and spin off into darkness. IT'S A NATURAL PROCESS as you expand your capacity and awareness, the world needs healing and we are here to do it individually, and then together collectively"

"Stillness for peace, answers, purpose, stability, knowledge, one must go within for all these things. Outside is just there to teach and then to bring within too. Then we bring what's inside, into the world. It's a game of give and take, or give and give; abundance shall be your reality then"

"The Spiritual part of is human is perfect, it is the human part that needs the experiences to help to refine itself slowly back into its original higher self. Going through stuff here is part of the package, and having the experience as part of your human self gives you the ability to help others, within this world and the universe."

"Take everything as a learning curve. You have experiences that were given as learning, so take it all as experience to help others. We cannot truly understand something unless we experience it directly. Use your power/experiences to be a force for good in the world, like a loaded gun, ready for action and always ready"

"You are far stronger with the divine part of you than anything; it is the power of God itself. Just know this and focus on that when you need to."

"I just became more self-aware knowing we have in us more power than any being of dark. You have nothing to fear or be anxious about, shadows are not real anyway and storm clouds like the thoughts of a mind, do not last long at all. You're powerful, very powerful, relax and stay centred. Every hour I remind myself and take a step back from the mini human me"

"We are Powerful Creators, **born in the image of the one creator**; Power of creation is our Gift for the world"

"We are far more than just human; we are spiritual beings having a human experience and not human beings having a spiritual experience"

"The path never ends. You will always be learning, growing and expanding. Every time you reach a new height of expansion, new doors will always open. For the path is infinite and that is what infinity is, infinite expansion in awareness, FOREVER!"

"I am proud of the wisdom that flows through a person from a higher power from time to time, it makes me smile to capture it and write it down. This wisdom is meant for us all, it comes from a higher power, it comes from God The Creator of all life, to improve this world and standard of life for all beings. THAT is why IT MAKES ME SMILE, THAT is also how and why this Book emerged, the rest is down to you"

"No single person owns this wisdom, I just birthed it into a world in need and its power depends solely upon the people it reaches and then their application of it, within their lives and within the world. All things came from the Great Creator and there too shall they return"

"Honoured are those brave souls stepping forwards into the light of the new dawn, pushing forwards step by step heading to The Hills of The Great Mystery, and holding up the Pillars of Hope for all. Our dreams and futures are carried by them, together we will join and share the weight. One day we shall all be joined together in the sun"

"Self-sufficiency, self-determination, and freedom of creative expression, the right to pursue our higher purpose and calling, gifted into the hearts of each of us by God The Creator"

*"Swim within the seas of wisdom

and divine mystery"*

"Vengeance is not a path of the light"

"Age does not denote wisdom"

"The journey and how you get there is the most important thing, not the destination itself"

"Embody all that which you wish to see, and feel, and experience in the world."

"Out of love, out of time, we are gems in an Ocean of Mystery. It is time to reclaim fully your Multidimensional Heritage"

"The Living Truth comes from inside yourself, guides and true allies will find you when emanating fully what you already are and have the potential to be"

"Only a fool reacts,

a wise man RESPONDS"

"BEING the LIVING TRUTH,

leads to freedom"

"Inner Peace is achieved by living your hearts purpose, the purpose of the Greater Deeper True Mind, with no resistance from the Human Personal Shallow Surface Ego Mind"

"Come from the perspective that your know nothing and nor does anybody, Live in FLUID AWARENESS of The Heart instead. We will not be trapped in mind illusions here"

"Do not hold any belief unless it is true to the Creator as being one, as then it contains infinite potential. By accepting and surrendering to your true identity, you will come to remember the higher parts of yourself"

"Make the message of Your Heart and its purpose, the Heart of your purpose and message"

"Man IS what he believes"

"Ascension is NOT AN EVENT,

it's a chosen process"

"Be Mindful of The POWER OF CONSCIOUSNESS you can PULL FROM YOUR AWARENESS EVEN NOW, that can help improve your state of being and the state of the whole world. For everything is within a state and you ALREADY HAVE EVERYTHING YOU NEED"

"When we stand together as a

UNIFIED HUMAN RACE

in all its full glory and wondrous splendour, we are INDOMINABLE"

"Those who are truly Powerful and Strong will always pull all those around them up to their own level. If this is not the case it is because they are living in a lower state of fear disconnected from their True Self and Deeper Greater True Mind"

"In any expression of learning within this world consciousness is always left at the door. Yet CONSCIOUSNESS is exactly where we need to be looking"

"Greatness Emerges when you step out of the way. TRUE POWER is thrust upon those who do not actively seek it with Mind, thus they have the heart capacity for it, they have the necessary restraint required and can handle it. Using it only to heal and do GREAT GOOD. However those who do seek POWER actively with Mind will be destructive in its application. Unable to receive it, lacking the capacity for the gift that they stole, they will bring great harm to themselves, the world and others."

"Everything is energy birthed from the movement of consciousness. THE WILL OF THE ONE. The Universe IS MUSIC"

"The SYMPHONY OF DESTINY

is in your hands"

"A life that is well spent is spent upon something that outlasts it"

"People fear and are scared of all the wrong things"

"CREATE beautiful good things, beyond the understanding of those forces who wish to control or stop them"

"God does not force anything upon any being on any level, in its infinite wisdom and its benevolence it always allows things to unfold naturally, for this is God's way. If force is used upon you on any level, it is not of God, it could even be said to be anti-God.

Thus one can easily discern those of God and those not of God. Those working in the best interests of Gods greater plan, who serve it and the human family as a whole, or those who masquerade as good, but serve only themselves"

"Cultivate thy wisdom and you will tread upon the paths of heavenly virtue. Practice, practice, practice daily and the Divine Well Spring of your Eternal Nature will spring fourth from your being unburdening your soul for all time."

"Dis-Union within themselves is the grim companion to which some people and beings carry. Men create their own sorrows and very few know how to help themselves in misfortune.

That is the Circle that blinds and binds humanity in circles, but it is the EPITOME OF STRENGTH to know how to help oneself in misfortune. UNIFY your BEING to alleviate this, UNITY OF SELF is The **RESOLUTION to ALL SUFFERING**"

"The future of the human race is one in which as more time goes on people will be forced into True relationship with their Higher Self whether they consciously choose it or not, due to outside events and too much inaction by the human as a collective whole. Events will seem so crazy, strange, dark and chaotic they will have to align with their True Selves and be an embodiment of their Inner Divine Self, utilizing fully their Deeper Greater Minds, just to survive. They will not have time to think, they will just have to DO"

"Reconnecting to the Deeper Greater Mind and being in true relationship with the Higher Self is the way many in the world are learning to navigate the changing circumstances, as change becomes ever increasingly faster on all levels and in all its machinations. We are Truly living in an EMERGING GALACTIC WORLD once more"

"As mankind's situation becomes ever more precarious and desperate emerging as Our True Self within this Domain will be the Saving Grace of each individual, collectively as a race and worldly as a planet"

"Mortals are divine by race,

so do not fear even fear itself.

"Embody and LIVE what I have shown you, healing YOUR SOUL you will be insured from manifold evil. Let these gifts and fruits of wisdom be a shining light and as they blend then infuse on to thee. Your Higher Self is now birthing into life, embodying itself into your consciousness and being. Use it as your Highest Guide AND LIVE IT WITHIN THIS WORLD"

"Building a healthy race of human's means creating a world of leaders who are true to the LAW OF UNITY/ONENESS. A human race, those who are not lost within a false identity, who's Ego's do not rule their heart, but who exist within their original true identity given onto them by God The Creator.

A race who follows their heart wholeheartedly, without question, finding peace in its Singular Truth and certainty. A race ruled by the Deeper Greater Mind and who are in true relationship with their Higher Self, and are an embodiment of it within this World."

"Each moment is an opportunity to build a NEW EDEN within our world"

"Step forwards fully into yourself,

Own it, own it all or others will"

"POWER BE THE PEOPLE"

"WAY OF THE WATER.

It is a REMINDER that we are within a VIBRANT LIVING OCEAN OF CONSCIOUSNESS. WAY OF THE WATER is how I LIVE. We are THE OCEAN in a drop, a drop within THE OCEAN. We are ONE. The ONE who is many, the many who ARE ONE.

We are not only within the OCEAN, but any separation from it is but an ILLUSION OF MIND. We are FLOW, we are AWARENESS. Be SHAPELESS, FORMLESS. No restriction or self -CREATED BARRIERS within. Hold no belief, only that which is true to THE LAW OF UNITY AND ONENESS. No division between you and THE PERCIEVED REALITY. Let the PERCIEVED REALITY AND YOU BE ONE. DISSOLVE YOUR X POINT (point of observation) FROM SPACE TIME. Erase your limited human identity and ALIGN with your TRUE IDENTITY. Perceive with

HEART AND BE INFINITE. Use and Embody THE TOOLS OF INFINITY.

For YOUR JOURNEY OF ONE. IMAGINATION, COMPASSION, LOVE (**L.**iving **O.**ne **V.**ibrational **E.**nergy), and anything with INFINITE ENERGY POTENTIAL, that is WHOLE and CREATES NO DIVISION. Division is a MIND PROJECTION; you have no need for such illusions. The only way to understand the infinite is to BE INFINITE.

When you use INFINITY TOOLS, such as LOVE, COMPASSION, IMAGINATION, you will FEEL and be AWARE of everything you need to BE. The VIBRANT LIVING CONSCIOUSNESS WITHIN will FILL YOUR HOLY GRAIL that is your human form.

When people ask how can something come from nothing? Where did God come from? Or who made the CREATOR? THEY fail to

RECOGNIZE THEY HAVE ALREADY BUILT AN X POINT OF OBSERVATION and they will create nothing but a PARADOX OF UNDERSTANDING. The MIND will never know the answer for it is finite and runs at a speed of only 24 frames per second. Never try to understand something infinite with a FINITE FILTER. Only the HEART can answer this for knowing is finite and will only go so far. A PARADOX is just a LIMITATION of a FINITE LENZE OF PERCEPTION. Paradoxes do not exist when you wilfully shift your perception TO YOUR TRUE IDENTITY. The HEART will provide the answer with FEELING, have faith it WILL FILL YOUR CUP. Do not underestimate the POWER OF BELIEF IN YOURSELF.

THOUGHTS and EMOTION are the TOOL we can use within THIS OCEAN OF CONSCIOUSNESS in which we live. They are THE PROGRAM LANGUAGE we can use to

COLLAPSE THE WAVE FUNCTION OF REALITY.

Life is a reflection of what you allow yourself to see, EMBODY TRUTH and the TRUE REALITY WILL PRESENT ITSELF UNTO THEE. You will be given spiritual experiences to match your expanded awareness. What does spiritual mean? It simply means TRUTH and outside of space time. You now need to get rid of the DIVIDE between what you perceive as NORMAL REALITY AND PARANORMAL. Two divided realities will not SERVE YOU ANY LONGER. Make your outlook of reality to include the paranormal as the reality in which you live, stay true to THE LAW OF UNITY AND ONENESS,(No illusionary MIND division in your perceptions).

Dreams and Reality are also ONE. We are the X POINT between all omnipresent worlds and realities, What does this mean? It means in our perception from a human perspective (X) everything that occurs on the other side of the veil of THE OCEAN OF ONE seems to occur simultaneously with no linear form, and what we perceive as past, present, future, imagination, or Dreams, is occurring all at once.

All timelines exist at once, both good and bad, everything you can imagine or are yet to imagine already exists in manifest form in the VIBRANT LIVING OCEAN OF CONSCIOUSNESS. Beyond the THIN MAGNETIC WALL of energy, we call OUR UNIVERSE. All timelines are already there and completed, there is only ONE NOW MOMENT. For TIME ITSELF IT ALSO ILLUSION.

People find it difficult to bridge the divide between their two worlds. (Perceived normal and paranormal) WAY OF THE WATER provides this bridge, BY MAKING THEM ONE."

"Our pain, sorrow, and tragedies are the winning of the war for SELF, embracing fearlessly with certainty of The Hearts Greater Deeper Mind, and without doubt, the Dark Abyss of the predatory universe, IS OUR REDEMPTION. Within this dream within a dream, growing through all of this, all the eras of man, all the evils of all the worlds and dimensions, pushing forwards and never stopping. This is what makes us STRONG, EVOLVES us and eventually brings us BACK HOME TO OURSELVES"

"We are all Gods in The Remembering, each human being contains the potential energy of the WHOLE within EVERYPART, for that is what a HOLOGRAM IS"

"What is coming towards you IS CONSCIOUSNESS ITSELF. We are aware of becoming aware.

EMBRACE IT"

"Make the Unknown, Known.

Make all that is Imagined, Real.

Make all that is Dark, Light.

Make the unseen, Seen.

Make all that is Impossible, Possible.

Then You Have a High Degree of Mastery over ***Conscious Creation****"*

"Consciousness always provides the tools it requires to go to the next step in its evolution, CONSCIOUSNESS HAS A PLAN"

"Finally we re-joined creation. Fully Unified Conscious Creators once more able to bend reality to our will and create with unshakable Focus and Patience, anything we do so conceive of and imagine"

"Address this dimension, by always paying attention to the time and the place where you are at. Always stay within the present moment both on a physical level and spiritual level. For Your Focal Point always DETERMINES YOUR REALITY"

"INTENTION is a FOCUS of your ATTENTION. Learn to Create FOCAL POINTS OF INTENT and then patiently manifest your creations"

"Intent creates the CONTEXT,

Attention creates the FORM,

Integrity BRINGS IT ABOUT"

"The stones are placed, the **seeds planted**.

The gates are open & the waters of life flow towards The Great Tree that sprouts all pure, untamed reality. From the Wisdom Realms Of Eternity and The Great Sea, Come forth The Masters Of The Heart & Of Destiny"

"Plants seeds of awakening within this garden that we have inherited. Use all your natural skills and abilities to make it a beautiful garden in which to live. Eden is a state of being contained inside yourself in every moment, even now as you read this. It is your job to manifest your dreams into this domain, anything you can imagine, you can create and more. Eden is a dream but we can all make it happen. When one or more people are involved in something, it is no longer a dream, but a reality.

RAISE EDEN"

"THE END.

Is just a NEW BEGINNING,

The journey always starts at the END"

Daniel is a property renovator/investor and lives in a small cottage in the Lincolnshire Wolds, in the UK, an area of outstanding natural beauty.

He enjoys nature, the countryside, and the natural rhythm of Earth, life, and the Universe itself. He loves stillness and practices this each day and upon each hour.

Each day he takes time out to go into Deeper Relationship with his Higher Self and allows his Greater Deeper mind to emerge, becoming a more powerful embodiment of it day by day. Within this Deep Sacred State of meditation, and sometimes spontaneously throughout the day or night, the Deeper Currents and Pearls of Wisdom that are received from the deeper sacred space within are written down as Gifts for all.

Wisdom of the Eternal was birthed forth from this deeper communication with God The Creator. It is a Revelation for all Times and All People. Use the Insights and Knowledge, apply it in your life and in the world well, for it was meant for you and Now you have received it.

"BE L((((O))))VE"

You can contact Daniel through his **email**, for Business enquiries

danielofdoriaa@gmail.com

or visit his

You Tube channel for more information.

https://www.youtube.com/user/danielofdoriaa

© & ℗ Daniel Dunn Enterprises 2017.

© Copyrights ℗ Artwork –

Daniel Dunn Enterprises UK 2017

All Rights Reserved © 2017

Printed in Great Britain
by Amazon